INDIVIDUALITY

INDIVIDUALITY.
BY ✝ CHARLES.
FRANCIS ✝ ✝ ✝
ANNESLEY ✝ ✝
VOYSEY. AND
PUBLISHED. BY.
CHAPMAN·AND
HALL: L^TD. LONDON
1915

PREFACE

I have written these chapters in the earnest hope of encouraging my fellow-men to believe and feel the creative spirit within each and every one, which while stimulating thought, leads on to mutual sympathy and true union. And so through the working of natural laws, we come to create that beauty which draws us onward and upward.

C. F. A. Voysey.

10 New Square
Lincoln's Inn, W.C.
March 18th, 1915.

CHAPTER I : Introduction

" This above all, to thine own self be true, and it must follow, as the night the day, Thou canst not then be false to any man."

Let us assume that there is a beneficent and omnipotent controlling power, that is perfectly good and perfectly loving ; and that our existence here, is for the purpose of growing individual characters. These are the propositions upon which all the following conclusions are based, and the fertile soil out of which our thoughts must grow. This basis of order, and singleness of purpose, will affect our outlook upon nature, and what use we make of her must always primarily depend on our attitude of mind towards her.

The painter who sees in the tree, the majesty and benevolence of its author, will charm us by his rendering of it, far more than he who regards it as blind force, although fully conscious of its physical beauty.

We may carry to a photograph of a tree our own sense of reverence for Nature's Master, but we expect the artist to awaken within our breasts the songs of praise he himself has felt. And likewise all manifestation of nature must shew this emotional quality, if it is to arouse our reverence and stimulate our higher nature. Reverence cannot be felt for anything that we regard as inferior to ourselves : and it is this sentiment of reverence which makes us generous to one another, and strengthens our comparative faculty, leading us to classify all things and all actions, thoughts and feelings. It enables us to form in the mind human ideas far in advance of our attainment, which act like charms alluring us ever onward and upward. It is the bedrock upon which all character is ultimately built. Self-respect and self-reliance are forms of reverence, being based as they are on our conceptions of ideal possibilities. Even the atheist finds he cannot get on without some form of reverence. He holds to an ideal ethical perfection in man, or some notion of happiness or utility :

8

But whatever it may be, it must be superior to himself. Hence it must follow that the ideas we hold of the prime object of reverence will for ever be developing, as we improve in our moral and spiritual insight. This fact we find illustrated in history over and over again. Man's ideas of the great first cause must be for ever growing nobler and purer, and are leading us more and more to shrink from cramping and confining definitions. Dogma is deadening to progressive thought. Fresh types of wonder and beauty are slowly revealed, giving promise of still further revelation. This limitless nature of our spiritual vision stimulates our reverence, far more than if we were to fix our minds on clearly defined forces and attributes. The familiar slowly loses its hold, hence the constant charm of a conception that suggests further possibilities.

The idea of extension is one of the mightiest powers with which we are endowed. However right we are, there remains the idea that we might be more so ; there is no finality to human

9

thought—extension is its law. But it seems, human extension and development takes place in alternating spiritual and material directions ; as when we sleep for a period, while our bodies being freed from our minds recover those forces that in our waking hours, are the handmaids of our thoughts and feelings. Thus a generation or so is devoted to material needs, and brings forth the engine and the motor and machines in all their manifold forms, making even man into a machine until he shall awaken to a more spiritual activity, and rising above the strengthened forces of his material nature he shall rejoice in a fuller manhood. Surely it is true that war arouses the nobler side of our nature while material prosperity drags us down to the more animal state. So, too, human suffering of all kinds has a softening and mellowing effect and stimulates the growth of all our virtues. Pain produces endeavour, and sorrow brings wisdom. Physical suffering is the parent of pity. We are driven by disease to discover the everlasting laws of nature. And suffering kindles our sympathy for the sorrowful, and wages war against selfishness. Dissatisfaction must precede all reform. And so we must overcome evil with good.

As all reforms are first born in one mind, it must be from individual thought and feeling that all progress flows. We know that restlessness and discontent are signs of movement. We are advancing most when most discontented with ourselves. And we are in that way driven to look for life's essentials, the stable forces of nature, and the most permanent qualities, in order that our building, whatever it may be, may endure. What then are these essentials if not the moral sentiments, spiritual ideas or thoughts having a reality more real than matter; as for instance, reverence, love, justice, mercy, honesty, candour, generosity, humility, loyalty, order, and dignity. These are the real objects of virtue and the common bonds of union between all men in all times and in all places.

Our minds expand with the contemplation of matters of universal interest, and fundamental ideas of lasting importance, while we are narrowed and checked in our sympathy by microscopic enquiry into personal taste and minor details of daily life, although be it remembered, the details of our daily life are the means by which, in great measure, the emotions can be aroused and cultivated, depending as they do on our faculty of comparison for their right effect and application. All questions must be brought before the bar of our reason ; and each man must assess their relative values according to his temperament, heredity and tradition—hence our differences and therefore our dependence one on another.

If we all had the same affections in like degree, there would be no exchange of ideas, and therefore no progress, and dependence and reliance upon each other would be impossible. Dependence kindles love between man and man—independence tends to stifle it. Difference involves friction, and friction involves heat, and heat is force.

A world without individual differences of mind and body is unthinkable.

12

Yet paradoxical as it may seem, we unite in the reverence and love we cherish for the moral sentiments, because in their varied degrees there is a common basis. It is therefore upon these faculties that individuality must be built.

Our interest in all ethical qualities and keen desire to cultivate any one of our emotions, is the determining factor in establishing our personality. The various degrees of love alone will distinguish one man from another, and so on through all the list of common sentiments, the difference between individuals is one, more of degree than of kind.

A devotion to truth, for instance, will lead the designer to gather his knowledge of form by making careful diagrams of flowers and plants, by drawing plans and elevations and sections, he will learn the true form of every part, with its structural relation of parts, and in a way quite impossible, if instead he were to set the flower in a vase before him, and draw it as seen in perspective, which is the usual method. It is far more valuable to have a knowledge of the rose's form than a more or less true record of one only of the many million aspects of it.

The desire for truth thus leads to the accurate acquisition of knowledge that will help in the expression of other qualities, such as order, dignity, reticence, control, grace, delicacy, and rhythm, and to these must be added harmony, sympathy, candour, and loyalty. We learn in this way the interdependence of parts, the laws of construction, and how one form helps another and is delicately related to it. Such knowledge stimulates the power of conceiving combinations of forms, in the mind's eye, and this creative power is the harbinger of progress, and the spirit that draws men up and on out of sloth and materialism into spiritual activity.

The ape-like effort to imitate the whole of a flower as it appears to the eye is hopeless and impossible to start with. You may produce a result full of pleasing effect ; but at best it must be faulty. Whereas, you can get much nearer the truth if you study form, colour, texture, light and shade separ-

14

ately. When this knowledge is stored in the mind, individuality has its opportunity of expressing afresh the facts so gleaned, together with individual emphasis of particular sentiments.

A reverent mind stored with knowledge gleaned in this way, from Nature at first hand, cannot fail to be refined thereby and to have a refining influence on others, particularly if his energies be applied to objects of daily life. The qualities of things would then absorb our interest more than modes of expression. Truth would attract us more than convention ; fact would dominate fashion. This kind of study does not lead to egotism, but is helpful in keeping the mind interested in the natural qualities of things. And mindful, too, of the hidden forces of nature. It is the unseen that is the glory of the seen. The thought and feeling behind all expression.

It is only when we cease to be mindful of the spiritual origin of Nature and become absorbed by its material qualities that we exaggerate the importance of the mode of expression, and value technique more than the thoughts and feelings we seek to express. A deeper feeling will lead us to greater technical excellence, but technical excellence will not necessarily lead to deeper feeling.

We easily learn to regard the visible world as material only, and lose sight of its spiritual qualities and significance. And in this way our own mental state becomes less and less spiritual. We can be lifted out of this morass by reviving thoughts of individuality. Such thoughts are greatly stimulated by the recognition of the undeveloped ethical qualities in animals and plants, that is the individuality in them. Many have felt a sympathetic pang akin to sorrow, at the sight of a fallen tree. Where there is power to suffer there must be a soul to be saved and purified by the suffering.

It is no great step for the imagination to take, to read in animals and flowers the good sentiments we find in man. To do so certainly increases our interest in and sympathy with animals and plants ; and if our interest is thereby increased, there is every chance that the work done in this state

16

of mind will suggest to others very similar thoughts and feelings, and will keep our work fresh in the hearts of men for generations to come, when our names may be forgotten. Like our Cathedrals, which still warm and inspire us though we know not who built them. Sincere thought and feeling is transmittable through things material, soul responds to soul. Cloister and stained glass, and many a painted canvas, soften and swell the heart. How else can we explain the emotions we receive from works of art ?

It is important to recognize the difference between knowledge and wisdom, viz., acquaintance with affairs and spiritual insight. All works of art may show these qualities to those who look for them.

Spiritual insight and the quickening of moral sentiments may come through us without our will, as divine intuition, but the knowledge of affairs like the intimate knowledge of a country, its people, and its customs, can only come through experience and intellectual effort, which involves will. Those who believe that Bacon was the author of Shakespeare's plays have therefore to prove, not that the latter was incapable of the spiritual insight shewn in the plays and sonnets, attributed to him, but that he could not have acquired the knowledge of affairs that the author of those works displays.

Intellectual culture is far more dependent on social and material conditions than is spiritual culture, and so we find individuality cannot be expressed by mere knowledge of affairs, but must rely mainly on moral sentiments and the exercise of reason, in order to establish personality. Hence we find no two minds will record the same facts in exactly the same manner : though making use of the same emotions they will differ in degree. Degrees of intellectual and spiritual culture have always existed, and mark the differences between men far more deeply and truly than any physical differences can do. Seldom do we find the mind and spirit in the same person on equal planes of development.

The scientific mind is often so absorbed with material facts that reason is allowed to slumber. Logical conclusions quite clear to the spiritually active mind, are lost on the materialistic investigator of matter. His conventional methods of enquiry are inapplicable to a spiritual outlook. Theologians will say science is against religion, but no truth can be harmful to any other truth. What is vital and true in the material world must harmonize and agree with all that is vital and true in the spiritual world. Each individual can, if he will, reason in both spheres and find agreement in all vital principles. It is collectivist dogmas and established formulas about which men fight. If the author of matter and spirit be all-powerful and all-good, it is strictly logical to say the verities in the material sphere must harmonize with those in the spiritual, and that no good mind would allow evil to exist except for a good purpose if it were all-powerful. We may conceive of evil being the result of man's misuse of his powers, and being in a state of development he must be imperfect, and his imperfection is to him evil, but to the Creator it may be a necessary part of His gift to

19

us of free will. And therefore a good in disguise. For by our blunders and mistakes we learn all virtues. No virtue could be known but for preceding sin, no light without darkness. And so in our struggle for sincerity against popular conventions we strengthen individuality. Each man who desires to have a clear mind of his own must think all these questions out for himself ; they cannot be settled by collective action. And it is a mercy it is so, for our personal views are of infinite importance in the moulding of character.

The most intellectually cultured minds are sometimes to be found sadly wanting in the love of truth. Selfishness and brain power are often hand in hand. Learning and wisdom are brother and sister, always related but never the same, compliments as necessary to each other as night and day. When undue thought is given to learning, wisdom, which is of the spirit, faints away into the background behind the marble fields of ancient history and the conventions of modes. Then " manners maketh man," instead of the mind and spirit of man making each his own individual manner.

It is necessary to refer to originality, because we so often find it confounded with individuality, although it is so different an impulse. Healthy originality, we believe, is the expression or manifestation of ideas and feelings in an unfamiliar manner. When aimed at for its own sake, or for the purpose of attracting attention to its author, it is to be condemned. But when natural and spontaneous, and obedient to the laws of fitness, it is pleasing and right. It needs to be restrained, for any excessive originality is vulgar ; that is, excessive in itself, and out of proportion in its relation to others. Much in the same way may individuality be vulgar, if it lacks just proportion, or arouses bad thoughts and feelings. Individuality that encroaches on the rights of others, violates our sense of love, justice and generosity. At every turn we find these feelings are called upon, so that only by appealing to our moral sentiments can we form a just estimate of the worth of any man's work.

As Ruskin said, " Good taste is a moral quality."

The personality which is expressed by mode may arise from ignorance of other modes ; or it may be the expression of self not clearly defined. As for instance, when a strong nature is struggling to manifest itself, the semi-conscious presence of latent force will sometimes lead to unconventionality in dress, which, when indulged in through vanity, or any sense of superiority, is contemptible, or when deliberately adopted for the purpose of advertisement.

It is amazing how conformity to fashion in woman's dress will lead people of refinement to make ridiculous guys of themselves, often distorting the proportions of their figure to the verge of the grotesque. And it is remarkable that where individual judgment has been allowed play, how invariably it shows a reverence for the human form ; and the natural figure becomes the keynote of the costume, which is more or less made to . harmonize with it. Other forms of individual expression are often

22

scornfully termed eccentricity, because they are unconventional. Such peculiarities often growing into habits from early efforts to be sincere. Shyness shows itself in strange ways, and is the painful disease of self-consciousness that individuality would help to cure.

Passing now to the consideration of tradition, about which artists have said and written so much. As we understand the term, it denotes that mode which is, or was, generally accepted as the best under its attendant circumstances.

Let us bear in mind that circumstances often change without changing the mode of expression, whereby the latter loses its quality of fitness. In days of mail, a coat of arms denoted the manner of man that wore it. The loss of fitness, to those who regard the law of fitness as divine, is a blemish and a violation of the sense of reverence. We see innumerable architectural features made use of, long after the circumstances that gave them birth have ceased to exist. Forms and symbols are retained, on sentimental grounds, and because of their associations, long after their meaning has been forgotten.

There are two very distinct types of mind that we must recognize in this connection. The one is mistrustful of self, and must have precedent or authority of some sort to lean upon, even though it be only blind custom. Persons of this type *must* have crutches. They are mostly conformists, and lovers of law and order. The other type is more independent,and enquires into the why and the wherefore, and will be found ready to change the mode to meet changed or changing conditions. These are the nonconformists, who tend most to individuality. They also may love order if they have reverence. The former type tends inevitably to collectivism. Conformity is the very essence of collectivism, as we can still see in the influence of Rome on our conduct in every-day affairs.

There are large bodies of men banded together, not for the improvement of character or the encouragement of individuality, but for the coercion of the multitude into preconceived modes and manners. A cry is now

24

raised for a certain style of architecture, which happens to be at the moment what is called " the English Renaissance," a style which was first introduced into this country at one of the most morally corrupt periods of the nation's history.

The wealthy had travelled and seen the beauties of foreign countries, and impressions received by them in their moral darkness were all of a materialistic nature. While appreciating the modes of foreign work, they were forgetful of the conditions of climate and national character, and expressions of emotion were not what they looked for, and love of truth was neglected. There were cultured architects of exquisite taste, like Sir Christopher Wren, who showed his fine sense of proportion, in the foreign tongue. He, no doubt, was quite unconscious that the accentuation of jointing of stone-work, known as rustication, was originally a deliberate attempt to deceive, it being adopted to make walls look more solid than they really were, a direct and immoral effort on the part of the originators, who were quite

25

prolific in that form of falsehood, and possibly like their imitators of to-day, were quite unconscious they were doing anything wrong.

It is inconceivable that so many of our leading architects at the present time should be reviving these samples of ancient sin, and, at the same time, believe them to be evil. Collectivism and conformity have made them mimic the manners of those they looked up to ; sincerity and honesty of expression has been dominated by fashion, and forms are now used for their material qualities only, regardless of their spiritual significance.

The return to the forms and modes of a corrupt period indicates that modes have lost their moral significance, and that men have become so materialistic that they cannot discern more than material qualities, so that buildings to them are nothing more than combinations of form, colour, texture, light and shade. Moral qualities are smothered by the parasite of materialism which has twined its tendrels about every branch.

How powerful conventions may

become it is easy to see. A style accepted by general consent is of the essence of a tyrant. Symmetry, for instance, will impose its iron law, and lead the architect to cover his library door with books, if the door by proclaiming itself should upset the symmetrical balance of the room ; surely that which requires fraud to defend it cannot be morally sound.

Multitudes of examples could be mentioned where candour, truth, and fitness are sacrificed to conformity to so-called style.

There are many straightforward and honest folk whose moral code is to conform to custom, without question ; their habit of mind is one of reliance on others, and they naturally fall in with any collectivist movement. They cannot be expected to act independently, having minds that are controlled from without more than from within.

Providence does work through the individual, but human passion only moves the crowd.

The condition of mind which is conscious of its own responsibility and recognizes the moral sentiments

27

acting from a fixed principle, cannot escape the sense of humility and dread of selfishness. Healthy individualism does not tend to self-righteousness or selfishness. On the contrary, it helps to eradicate those faults, while selfish thoughtlessness is practised by blind obedience to custom.

What must be emphasized is the fact that individuality forces intelligent enquiry into our mental state, and leads to its development by turning the attention inwards, and so stimulating the spiritual activities. This self-culture should lessen the tendency to find fault, and increase our readiness to make excuses for others.

A quickened sense of reverence will lead us to respect the seasons and the natural qualities of materials ; and we shall then avoid things that look better than they are, or are pretending to be different.

The great flood of commercialism has made men follow one another, on collectivist lines, to secure a given end ; and has been fruitful in its fashions for change and artificial excitement, and has fastened our attention on the material gain to such an extent, that we are ready to sacrifice everything else for it, and are not even conscious of the lack of reverence it engenders.

We travel abroad, ignoring as far as possible all climatic and national differences. If nature is proving the fitness of any plant for any particular place, we must needs transplant it, and so far as possible obliterate all that is local and fitting to its birthplace.

Countless instances there are of customs which, when intelligently examined, are found to be indefensible, and though harmless in the main, they form the habit of sheep-like following, and retard progress and weaken the sense of individual responsibility.

We do not rely on one theory to explain all ills, and in defending individualism, we remember collectivism may have its place and its advantages. But if we would train character and preserve individual responsibility, we must most jealously guard individualism. Especially in these days, when the State has degenerated into a machine for producing armies of officials, with volumes of rules and regulations stereotyped and settled to suit given conditions, which by the laws of Nature must be for ever changing and developing. With the present formalism, no latitude is left to expanding intelligence. And sentiment is looked on as quite outside the pale of practical politics.

Do we not recognize in all business transactions how the charm of human feeling, human sympathy, and variety of outlook are vastly more helpful, than the collectivist rules and regulations of committees ? Who would not rather deal with one man than with a firm ? A little reasoning and generous give and take will often adjust differences, to the mutual benefit of contending parties—difficulties that established rules and regulations only make impossible of solution. In other words, individual control is more elastic than State control, and more elevating to the character.

Combination increases the power of government while decreasing personal responsibility, and so it happens that companies will often pursue conduct which individual members · of the governing body would shrink from. Such unions also establish conventions and modes which when clearly formulated and imposed stifle individual effort and development.

Collectivism becomes a most powerful agent in the controlling of matter, since our lower nature, relying on material rather than spiritual forces, responds more readily to material treatment. The more spiritual are more amenable to persuasion. Personal influence will lead rather than drive. Individuality, then, is on the side of winning co-operation, while collectivism is for compelling obedience. And none will deny that it is better to lead men through their affections than drive them through their fears.

The love of sincerity and truth is the mainspring of individuality ; it is the secret of the impulse to have all around in harmony with mind and heart. The desire for home is born of this holy impulse. And step by step we see how the old home instinct grew out of sincerity ; until to-day we have developed the conflict between

31   c

the man who says, " I want to have a house to suit myself ; I am paying for it, and therefore have a right to dictate to him who is to fashion it." And the conscientious architect is staggered at the situation. He, too, has to satisfy himself, trained as he is in conventions, his ideas are sure to clash with those of the individual home lover, unless a common basis of agreement can be found. Surely, then, if requirements and conditions are carefully studied, the sentiments common to all will form the leven, and truth, candour, directness, dignity, and grace will make any home attractive without reference to any modes of building, either ancient or modern. Or any loss of self-respect on either side. It can never be necessary for the faithfulness of one to sacrifice the fidelity of another. Wherever such conflict appears necessary, there must be want of understanding, or the influence of conventionality and slavish observance of established modes. The impulse to be faithful is common to all, and divinely ordained, therefore it cannot be self-destroying. Faithfulness is not

32

only the rule of individuality but the bond of union between man and man. The collectivist looks for fidelity to the rules of his society, from every member, not stopping to study the particular motives behind each membership. Each political party leader expects loyalty to his party unquestionly. The confidence so established must be very limited, whereas fidelity to a principle of conduct established in the heart and unsupported by fears of worldly penalty, must establish the feeling of faithfulness when discovered, far more firmly than any conduct that is forced on us by fear. Hence to obey the dictates of conscience, however misguided be the judgment, is nobler than the slavish conformity to the conventions of collectivism, or to the laws laid down by a party leader.

CHAPTER II
COLLECTIVISM

CHAPTER II : Collectivism

"It is the universal law that whatever pursuit, whatever doctrine becomes fashionable, shall lose a portion of that dignity, which it had possessed while it was confined to a small but earnest minority, and was loved for its own sake alone."—(Macaulay).

Collectivism, convention, and fashion, all derive their power through the suppression of the individual. Men's minds and bodies are forced into grooves and moulded into machine-like order; being banded together like soldiers for a common purpose, their united efforts gather accumulating strength.

Collectivism must then be judged by the aim in view, and cannot be regarded as a general principal to be lightly adopted. Like all physical force, it will work for good or ill with equal facility ; thus only when we know the aim is good, can we uphold the system. Individuality being the basis of character, collectivism can have but little effect that is not harmful to its development. Conduct can be controlled by collective action, but conduct is not character, nor is it always the result of character. Collectivism is a form of compulsion that cannot have the same ethical value and effect on character that individual free choice must always have. It requires but little effort to swim with the stream, and slide almost unconsciously into the modes and manners of the multitude. We become easily satisfied with a standard more or less defined and established in the mind, whereas the individualist's standard is ever evolving towards a greater perfection.

Many speak and act as if multitudes of men were incapable of self-culture and that therefore collectivism is necessary, and clearly defined lines of action must be imposed upon them. But against definite restriction to individual liberty men have fought in all times. And yet is it not quite possible to agree, that Government should confine its forces to the protection of the weak against the strong, leaving every man to work out his own salvation in the domain of thought and feeling ?

We have no right to assume that large masses of men are depraved, or incapable of self-culture. The idea has given rise to all manner of laws that degrade rather than elevate. Moral sentiments are not always recognized as universal, and hence it is we tyrannize over one another. It would seem that if every man is blessed with the same fundamental sentiments, and our differences are only those of degree, much more can be accomplished by persuasion than by force, and by taking for granted that every man has the feeling we should desire to cultivate. If then liberty of thought is essential to the growth of character, combined coercion of any kind which limits thought must check its development. Furthermore, the great danger of collectivist action is in the acceptance of a given idea as final, and fixed in its value ; silencing the individual conscience and discouraging personal criticism and enquiry. It also presents a beaten track to the idle traveller who shirks the strain of a rugged way.

39

Conduct controlled by custom petri-
fies intelligent reasoning and creative
enterprise, and leads us to act like
machines with the inevitable neglect
of all esthetic thought. All personal
feeling is suppressed, and sincerity is
not called upon ; therefore Collectivism must enslave, and while killing
individuality makes men more materialistic. It also accentuates class differences and encourages prejudice, hence
sects are multiplied and contentions
ensue. Theories are tried by cliques,
and often become discredited by their
power to attract the thoughtless and
superficial. For example, garden sub-
urb societies spring into being, and
gather a certain class of mind that
responds to the principle theory of the
society, but in time the union becomes
limited by the exhaustion of energy.
Great reforms are expected when two
or three are gathered together, but
disappointment invariably follows.
The fascination of having our thinking done for us is very real to minds
already jaded by materialistic interests,
and so the needs of the flesh will
jostle out the thoughts of the spirit.

And thus we find collectivism most powerful in relieving us from personal responsibility and anxiety. We require little mental effort in obeying established habits, and after a time become more automatic in thought and action. It is a kind of lathe process that turns off all individual knots and angles, and smoothes us all down to one standard pattern.

It is difficult to persuade others that pain is a blessing in disguise, that the struggle that strains is strengthening, that to enquire of oneself the why and the wherefore of all our likes and dislikes is immensely helpful, and stimulating to reason and justice. Creative artists must go through this process of reason, if they would avoid becoming slaves to pure innovation and the prey of fashion mongers. Many architects of to-day say in effect, " let us have an established mode, a national style of architecture. Save us from the individual, who, if left alone, will shock our prejudices, and violate our established ideas. The standard of past ages is good enough for us and must be kept up, even at the sacrifice of living men. What care we for the development of human faculties for future good, by the side of dead records of dead men. Let us make the mode of a man or a period the fashion. Let newspapers and stump orators take up the jargon of styles, and then see how we shall be saved from difficult analytical criticism, and assisted by having a fixed standard for all taste, and a method of work, within the capacity of the meanest intellect. It is the old trades union tendency to provide one dead level of mediocrity in order that the feeble may fare as well as the famous.

This cry for the regulation of our architecture (for a ministry of art) is only one instance of the regulation we are seeking in every other walk of life : it is the collectivist tendency, as opposed to the individualistic. By this method it is thought to save the pain and trouble which must be bravely met, and even welcomed by those who would grow strong and stand alone.

We are so much occupied with combining for material ends, that it is almost hard to be patient with the individualist; but the time is fast approaching when the pendulum will swing the other way, and the mind on the lower side (that is, the individual more or less out of tune with his time) will have to induce the upward movement in the other direction, and so we shall find that the last shall be first, and the first last. Being out of tune with your time, if it does not mean madness, may mean getting into tune with the next: and anticipating the thought and feeling of the future.

Collectivism has instituted the hall mark which is indeed a useful badge that saves the County and Town Councillor from the danger of losing his seat. In spending public money, what a comfort it must be to him to appeal to the magic sigh, and say for instance, "Is not this competitive design something like St. Paul's?" and the general standard, however low, is accepted when an individual standard whole heavens higher would be regarded with fear and trembling. Collectivism is the coward's cloak.

This system by which all our public

43

buildings have been produced during the last generation or so, is deeply degrading to the individuals who compete; instead of evolving the character of each edifice out of requirements, and conditions, moulded in sincerity with hearts set on moral sentiments; the mode or style thought to be favoured by the authorities is assumed and set up as the keynote of the design to which all requirements and conditions must be tuned. The design, instead of proceeding from within outwards, is forced from without inwards. Collonades and cornices that have done duty for temples, town halls, and theatres, or clothed our public baths, banks and Baptist chapels, crop up everywhere, being compressed or extended to fit the size required. This standardizing is, no doubt, good for the immediate profits of trade, but it will not make men mentally or spiritually better. The system that crushes individual sincerity cannot bring lasting credit to any community.

CHAPTER III : Education

When education was regarded as the general cultivation of character, and the drawing out and development and stimulation of latent qualities, such as the moral sentiments, a standard curriculum would doubtless prove adaptable to all who could afford the luxury. But a more materialistic tendency has changed our ideas of education into the teaching of modes and manners, and matter is made to dominate spirit. Education is required as a means to wealth and authority. And the class of student to-day is as varied as the grasses of the field. Age culture and environment vary to such an extent that the training suitable to one class is quite unsuited to another. This has led to specialization and the suiting of lesson to learner as far as possible. Individual capacity seems to be more thought of than formerly. And its consideration should lead us more and more to see its importance, and the enormous value of personal effort and conflict. To be driven to make up the mind for oneself, and feel the responsibility of so doing, is essential to the development of character. Parents too often forget that children grow up, and are too apt to rely on rules and regulations, forgetting that Englishmen who pride themselves on their common sense, are only encouraged to cultivate it by having confidence placed in them. Youths are either crushed into servility or driven to rebellion if confidence is not freely accorded them. Expect the best, and you are more likely to get the best out of others. The collectivist principle does not seem to readily admit of this treatment.

It becomes necessary to fix a standard when large numbers have to be marshalled for any purpose, which must result in the neglect of individual qualities : the particular is ignored for the sake of the general, and this leads to a classification that tends to the social elevation of the unfit, while lowering the social status of the fit ;

48

breeding anarchy on the one side and feeble followers of fashion on the other. When education is regarded as a means to the accumulation of wealth and power, when we say certain things should be learned because they are useful, we are forgetting that the cultivation of character is far more important than any worldly success, it being only character that enables us to use or enjoy material things wisely. We must distinguish between emotional qualities and modes of expression ; but if we do not, the effect of beauty on the mind is smothered by the pride in its possession, and the costly vase is valued because it reflects the owner's material qualities, instead of for its own refining influences. Then books are read for entertainment rather than for the cultivation and stimulation of our higher nature.

Spiritual culture cannot be tested by competitive examination like mathematical knowledge, and so, in a materialistic world, little counts that is not marketable, while visible proofs of information are desired far more than right thinking and feeling.

49

To the spiritually cultured the effect of beauty or ugliness in things is quickly recognized ; beauty is courted because it begets beauty, but to the materialistic mind ugliness is to be tolerated if not actually harboured. We are advised that it is fussy and vexatious to object to the unpleasant shapes and colours of the objects around us. Stony indifference to ugliness is looked upon as good mannered. The influence for good or ill on the character of such studied indifference is not in the least observed. It would be well to ask ourselves, if we are courting the arts only to be entertained, and in consequence feeding our selfish instincts and missing the real benefits of their influence. We should seek beauty in our surroundings quite as reasonably and fervently as we seek fresh air and golf ; but while the body is our first consideration, our meat will come to us on ugly plates.

Great advantage might accrue if the apprenticeship system could be revived and made to curtail the wholesale and promiscuous state training of multitudes who find, to their sorrow, that there is no demand for the powers they have laboured so hard to acquire.

Under the apprenticeship system, not only special instruction is given, but what is often more valuable, the influence of the master's personality silently and insiduously cultivating the moral sense of his pupil, and so fitting him for any occupation that economic conditions might dictate. This method is more one of drawing out than cramming in, and the personal element must make a more lasting impression on the mind than any school or college training.

May it not be truly said that the reason why old soldiers so often make good servants, is due to the fact that they have been trained in reverence, order, loyalty, and justice. And by example from their officers have imbibed many qualities that can only be transmitted through direct personal influence and contact. Though the idea of an army is collective in its inception, in its working it is very individualistic. The sense of relation

51

is well preserved, and personal responsibility is always maintained in its healthiest aspect, viz., the unit's relation to the multitude. Men, by being made soldiers, are not necessarily made machines, nor are they made egoists. But in many trade movements the one aim being gain, no ethical influences are allowed to operate, and a large body of workers are in consequence reduced to mere machines. Self-respect and reverence are smothered by greed. In wild country districts you may often discover that the sweet human qualities are much nearer the surface. You can safely venture a friendly remark to a workman about his work, if you are far enough away from a town, but in any city it would be hazardous.

Early training would have a greater humanizing effect if it encouraged the moral sentiments more than emulation in modes, and a more extended interest in spiritual affairs, would soon dispel the horror that the materialist now feels at the very mention of the names " Moral " or " Spiritual." It does seem a pity that ethics should

52

be delegated to any particular class of men, or any special place or time, for they concern us all at all times, and in all places. It should be possible to inculcate moral sentiments without sickening the student. The modes of various businesses and conduct of affairs, as well as arts and crafts, could be made a powerful agency for propagating and stimulating individuality. And by these means men could be weaned from materialism to a more spiritual state of mind. It has only been in periods of great spiritual activity that the arts have flourished. And always at such times there has been a greater tendency towards individuality rather than collectivism.

Too often we hear the remark that " sentiment has nothing to do with business." The statement betrays the fact that in early life men learn to separate their characters, and live two lives. One which has a moral purpose, and one which is purely material. Instead of which we ought to combine the two, and so remain more conscious of the moral significance of all matter, mindful, too, that matter is merely

53

the vehicle for the expression of thought and feeling, and the schoolhouse of character. Whatever it be, it must bear some relation to human character, and it must manifest the spirit of man as Nature manifests the spirit of God. Nothing exists as a thing apart, and by pressing this point continually we work on the individual through himself, to the multitude, and stimulate the control that is from within, rather than from without, thus checking collectivism and tyranny.

Would it not be well if we could persuade the painter that, being blessed with delicate feeling and true sight, giving him power to create beauty of form, colour, texture, light and shade, it is not right that he should confine those qualities in gold frames, and shut his eyes to the moral significance of things around him and live content in the midst of ugliness. The love of beauty should include everything that makes our lives more beautiful. The artist's talents are cramped and confined by the collectivist banding and branding. Do not painters get branded as painters of cows or clouds, sea or subject ; and different crafts are separated until we get sculpture without colour, painting without design, and architecture without either. It is time the artist set himself to stimulate the layman by showing a keener interest in objects of daily use. And let him come off his pedestal and make his coal-scuttle beautiful.

Collectivist methods of dealing with material conditions exclude the consideration of individual character ; thus the mind is for the time being left in the background. And the more materialistic we become, the more material conditions grow in importance. All class differences become magnified, whereas if we would pay more attention to harmony and likeness, we must think more of the common emotions and encourage more active spirituality. Individuality in a healthy state is a sure aid in this direction. Briefly stated, the more spiritual we are the greater the possibilities of union between man and man. But the more materialistic we become, the more are our differences manifest.

55

Differences of degree in moral sentiments are not only a healthy stimulus
to progress, but they make intercourse
both possible and necessary. Whereas
differences of material condition tend
less to harmony than to discord.
Absolute likeness in material condition
could only be possible to men of equal
moral and spiritual culture. Such
equality, we know, has never existed,
and can never exist, because it would
be contrary to the laws of Nature ;
the essential foundation of personality
being unlikeness. We are made conscious of our own personality by
observing our difference to others.
How, then, can we ever hope to give
equal opportunities to all men ? And
hence we find what is one man's meat
is another man's poison, and each has
to find out for himself wherein his
capacity lies. To encourage a child to
teach itself would seem the highest
achievement of education, and this
can surely be done only by stimulating
ethical thought. It cannot be denied
that nothing in this world is worth
caring about in comparison with our
thought. Thought must direct our

feeling, therefore it must come first, although our noblest deeds are often done intuitively and, as it were, before we have time to think ; yet who can say that these impulses are not the rewards of previous good desires, and the outcome of spiritual longing. We often find ourselves performing little acts quite unconsciously, as the habit of winding up one's watch. So the benevolent impulse can be trained to act automatically by sincere desire to cultivate it in the heart. Many of us can say with truth, " what my father was has taught me more than what my father knew." So our education ought to run on ethical lines, and cultivate individual rather than collective effort, and lead us through self-culture to unselfishness.

CHAPTER IV

MODES HELPFUL TO THE
EXPRESSION OF INDIVIDU-
ALITY

CHAPTER IV. : Modes helpful to the Expression of Individuality

Gothic architecture grew out of the careful consideration of requirements and conditions, and obedience to the natural qualities of materials ; in fact, all the best building throughout the world has grown in that way, and was ever so created, until men became corrupted by materialistic ideas, and then the mode of expression was regarded as more important than the conditions and requirements with which they were dealing. The fascination of the mode of a Grecian Temple led to the endeavour to adapt it to a mansion house. Individual grappling with conditions and requirements by men of lofty moral sense, has given us the finest and purest architecture. A reverence for climatic and other natural national conditions spiritual, as well as material, has produced in this country its glorious cathedrals, colleges and Tudor houses.

Could we but revive the individualistic spirit and stimulate moral sentiment, then, with requirements and conditions clearly before us, we should once more have a noble national architecture, without any revival of any particular style, either native or foreign. Certain conventions, dictated by a complete knowledge of material and needs, would naturally lead to the use of many familiar forms. The principles of the lintel and the arch, which are based on material qualities, must for ever remain true principles. But if we cast behind us all preconceived styles, our work will still possess a style, but it will be a living natural and true expression of modern needs and ideals: not an insincere imitation of other nations or other times.

The tyranny of imposing a mode of expression in any of the arts must seriously check individual sincerity and lead to an indifference to truth, which is the most corrupting of influences.

Men cannot be honest while imitating the sentiments of others which they often neither feel or understand. It is because we are not trying to be sincere in our building, not aiming at individuality, but are dominated by collectivism, that our Public Buildings are so dumb and death-like ; many have the qualities of good proportion, clever, ingenious construction, sensible use of material, and such like charms, but for the expression of living sentiment and spiritual force— such as our old houses and cathedrals present—they are silent, dead, soulless piles of mortifying insincerity, which only sadden us.

The lack of noble sentiment in our modern buildings is due to the materialism of the age, which has led to the assumption of a foreign style, and the acquisition of material qualities only. Thought and feeling are ignored, hence the works are still-born. Individuality is not called for, but conformity to old conventions and standard modes are imposed by collective opinion. We are not allowed to work out our own salvation, but must tread the road that is easiest for the duffer.

Democracy, as it becomes more

articulate and better organized, becomes more mechanical, and less able or willing to recognize individuality. Convention relieves the individual from thought and anxiety. We say "there is safety in numbers," and that in a multitude of councillors there is great wisdom. But this false philosophy is itself the outcome of fear, and must be uprooted before we shall acquire true independence and manly courage.

Our domestic architecture has advanced much more than that of our public buildings, because we have cast off the tyranny of styles, and refused to be hampered by any preconceived mode. While devoting the whole mind to meeting most fitly, all the existing requirements and conditions ; on the other hand, unfortunately, materialism has led to the consideration of material fitness only. For their homes many people say, " Give us personal ease and comfort— we do not want sentiment." The styles as taught in the schools have been gradually discredited in the search for greater fitness, and the

64

process was greatly accelerated by the introduction of machinery, which has revolutionized our methods of production, construction and design.

Of course, we look not for dignity in the front door while struggling to make it look better than it is. If it is not oak, must it not be painted to look like it ? Were individual conscientiousness more appreciated, the artist would be allowed greater freedom, instead of as now being treated as a tradesman and paid hireling, who's duty it is only to carry out instructions and make good bargains.

While artists are fully alive to all practical considerations, and are ready to meet all requirements and conditions imposed upon them, recognizing such as the best foundations for design, there is still left a wide field in which the emotions can, and should, operate to the mutual advantage of all. It is only blindness to these qualities that has led to the servility of art workers. To save his pocket he has often to lose his soul. Frankness is not to his worldly advantage. It has not always been so,

nor can it for long remain. Our spirits
must have an awakening, and we must
see that the imposition of any style,
dictates a mode of expression false
and foreign to the designer, and the
employment of forms, originally in-
tended to deceive the eye, violates
the conscience and vitiates the taste.

It has often been observed that the
architecture of a people, must always
be a true reflection of their moral and
spiritual condition. And in an age
where you find a prolific display of
deceptions, you may be sure that the
people are more materially than spiritually advanced, and more collectivist
than individual.

In early Tudor times the aristocratic
idea was more alive than it is to-day,
and there was in consequence much
patronage of individuals. Moral sentiments were then as fashionable as
motor cars are now.

Another mode helpful to the growth
of individuality, and all its attendant
blessings, would be the removal of all
doctrinal restrictions from men when
in the pulpit. But we must not pursue
this thorny subject, as many will think

66

the mere mention of it is enough to condemn individuality altogether.

Nevertheless our zeal for freedom of thought grows out of a reverence for truth and faithfulness ; and, while the cultivation of ethics must involve the recognition of law and order, loyalty is only possible to the free mind. Obedience you may have from the slave, but loyalty a man can only bestow freely, and it is an addition to, not a part of, his obedience.

Many are the channels through which the ship of personality may navigate, and multiform the winds of emotion that blow hither and thither, safety only being possible while one mind holds the helm. You may lead and encourage the Captain by kindness, which cannot weaken responsibility, but never must external authority usurp the throne. We must see more and more clearly the difference between obedience to an inner monitor and conformity to outside pressure, whether proceeding from one or many, and this perception will make us recoil more and more from collectivism.

The study of dress is very illumin-
ating to this question of individuality.
Instinctively we feel the outward
semblance of equality as conducive
to social intercourse, hence the fashion
for dressing all men like waiters when
they are to dine together. And it
would seem, that the desire to hide
material differences is the underlying
principle of all uniforms. It is the same
for large bodies of men required to
express unity of purpose. The Military
and Naval uniforms enhance the effect
of terror and apparent power of an
enemy. It is a splendid institution
even for bank clerks, or Stock Exchange men. There can be no harm
in having them labelled with silk hats.
But there is yet a fascination in per-
ceiving the difference of vocation in
differences of dress ; and the more
attention the individual gives to his
own costume, the more enlightening
it becomes. He cannot disguise his
temperament or help telling you if
his sympathies are more with a period
in history than with the grace of
Nature. He will conform or not to the
fashions of those he respects, according

68

to the power of his own sentiments. A natural shyness, and desire not to attract attention, will lead him to suppress his personal feeling almost to extinction. More powerful still is the inclination felt by the individualist, to differentiate : fashions will be avoided by him which he finds favoured by those socially beneath him. This is a natural instinct often found operating quite unconsciously.

The point most worthy of attention, however, is not a question as to the relative values of uniformity or variety ; but an enquiry as to how to influence the development of any costume, so as to make it a benefit to personal character. At present it seems mainly governed by commercial considerations.

If, however, dress is to be regarded as a means of culture, as well as a protection, and an affair of commerce from the production of which millions get their living, moral sentiments will have to be acknowledged and taken into account much more than they are at present. Reverence, truth, honesty, candour, generosity, humility, order, and directness will have to dominate and suppress the collective energy of change-mongers. Human machines for stimulating human wants are very good for trade, and help men to amass wealth. If wealth is our sole aim, there is no more to be said ; but if our aim is the cultivation of character, greater individuality will conduce to greater sincerity ; and any dislocation of trade that might follow from the suppression of collectivism, would be amply compensated by the general culture accruing. It cannot be doubted that, but for fashion, men and women would take keener delight in beautifying costume. Interest in the grace and loveliness of forms, colours, and textures of everyday life must work magic on our characters, and send into oblivion much of our sordid materialism. Change the motive for our dressing, from competitive rivalry into an act of reverence towards the body, expressive of the higher qualities of mind, and you then convert costume into a means of culture and minister of beauty. Individualism, then, is the main cure for the present ugliness of dress, and the more we tend to follow fashion, the more collectivist we shall become; and by aiding the commercial instinct in the tradesman, we starve to death those sentiments we all value, and would gladly encourage.

Recognition in the mind of individuals, of the moral significance of all humanly created things, is all we ask for. It ought not to be necessary to write or speak about such a matter. It is so powerful a force that one marvels that it is so commonly neglected, and so often absent from the mind altogether. The spirit of man requires nourishment as much as his body; and yet how content many of us are to starve our spiritual nature, and cultivate a calm endurance of the ugliness around us.

It is interesting to note how some modern scientists are beginning to show a restless discontent with materialism pure and simple, and are seeking to articulate the divine impulse of the spirit.

We long to see it demonstrated and accepted by all men that the spirit behind all matter is more loveable than matter itself ; and, while it cannot be handed from one to another, it is to be possessed by all. Through individual thought and feeling we shall see, and create, what collectively we can only defile.

CHAPTER V
HOW INDIVIDUALITY TENDS TO UNION

CHAPTER V : How Individuality tends to Union

It is often said that the artist must express himself, by which bald statement it is, we suppose, meant that he should give expression to all his personal idiosyncracies, and strive for self-assertion in every direction ; but it is surely possible for him, while remaining absolutely sincere, to forget himself and lose his conscious identity in the endeavour to express those thoughts and feelings and those qualities of character which are of universal interest, and understood by all men. We must first and foremost demand from the artist that he be sincere ; his own temperament and sense of proportion he cannot get away from— they must influence his work at every turn, but should not be his motive for addressing us.

To enjoy working thoroughly we must be creating something, even if it is only the sense of order. And to create beauty for others is a joy that must subdue the desire for self-assertion.

The carvers of miserere seats and gargoyles, in ancient times, were full of merry delight in the common interests of their own times. Moral sentiments (sometimes immoral) were of general interest, and absorbed all their time. They did not speculate in fantastic modes of expression, like the cubists and post impressionists ; their playful fancy and pathetic moods told of everyday events and common interests : what their brothers thought and felt and did was enough, and they kept beneath their heel all tendency to parade their technical skill or personal peculiarities.

Sensuality has been a human quality more or less pronounced in every age, but excessive devotion to *sensuous* emotion has only been possible in periods of profound materialism. Not until moral sentiments were obscured, was such work as that of Beardsley and Whistler made popular ; for sensuous feeling is dependent on matter, and hence the increased interest in it in a materialistic age.

76

Many artists contend that sensuous qualities, represented with good taste and good technique, are all that need be demanded in a work of art. But these qualities alone appeal only to the expert and sensuously inclined. Whereas, if in addition to sensuous qualities emotional thoughts are aroused, and the higher side of our nature is appealed to, the effect is far more general and deeper and wider in its power to refine. And so individuality, expressed in common sentiments, tends to a community of interests and universal sympathy, while representations of material and sensuous qualities will appeal only to comparatively few.

Clearly defined limitations of interest must lead to collectivism and ultimate stagnation ; mutual admiration societies are short lived. The rate at which we live tends to specialization ; we feel we have time only for a tithe of the multitude of pursuits, and so, tending towards collectivism, we become divided in interest, and band together to further our own particular ends. Only the studious

77

cultivation of individualism by the stimulation of moral sentiments, will save us from becoming narrowed and disunited, sectarian and unsympathetic.

We welcome every movement of society that will strengthen and refresh the sentiments that man can neither give nor take away, that are our precious inheritance subject to our care, but not to out disposal—those spiritual ideals that are everlasting and universal, for only these can keep us from degrading fear.

Moral perception must increase, as man's spiritual eyesight grows keener, leading him to avoid stereotyping standards ; ideas must have room to grow, each generation must put aside the idols of the past and purify its conception of those of the future. Natural religion is therefore based on morality, and expands with it—the purer the heart the higher will be the conception of the great first cause. This is a purely individual process. While collectivism binds men to definite ideas and ceremonies, we must acquire true union by personal effort to reach a common goal, and not by

78

collective submission to popular modes, or yielding to the pressure of numbers. The forces of custom that sway us weaken rather than strengthen character. The idea that great numbers of people need the control of custom, or some form of external authority is often very harmful in its effect. Self-reliance is not encouraged by denying the capacity for self-control, while to credit others with such qualities stimulates them. You may make a child a liar by calling him one, but encourage him to be truthful by reliance on his word.

We feel a natural respect for tradition : the reverence in those who value it is healthy and right, but when it is exercised to check men's efforts towards greater fitness and improved modes of serving their own time, it becomes a dangerous enemy to progress. Reverence for the past is admirable when exercised by the individual for his own guidance, but mischievous when imposed upon others. The experience gained by others in the possibilities and limitations of materials is most valuable, and will save loss of time and energy. Material qualities discovered and classified by those that have gone before us may fitly win our reverence and respect. Conduct may justly be imposed in many cases, but thought and feeling never. If our work is entirely material, the mode may well be dictated by another ; but the moment we introduce thought and feeling into it, we know that sincerity and truth demand freedom for the worker. Very little work in this world, if any, is of a purely material nature. Even the crossing-sweeper will show you some moral quality in his work : thoroughness, or order, or the absence of such qualities.

Trades unions, by limiting the individual enterprise of workmen, in regulating the number of bricks to be laid in a day's work, interfere unduly with the workman's sentiments, much to his degradation ; which fact alone is an eloquent example of the evil resulting from collectivism. The object of the unionist is, of course, to secure material advantage to his trade as a whole ; it clearly does not

80

produce unity. Privately appeal to the bricklayer's moral sense and he will respond at once, and see the advantage to himself and others of cultivating individual enterprise and self-respect. He, no less than we, desires not to be tied down to the low level of mediocrity. He must see that such a process divides men, and can never unite them in any true sense.

Collectivism among artists has circumscribed their sphere of usefulness to such an extent that subjects of discussion interesting to one branch have ceased to be attractive to the rest. A talk on architecture, for instance, attracts few painters, and so the brotherhood among the arts is cramped and confined, because the prevailing materialism bases the chief interest in the several branches of art, on their mode instead of on the thoughts and feelings which each has to express.

Apart from any literary motive, closer attention to individual feeling, would betray the various values placed on sentiments, and would, we think, form a closer bond of sympathy between artists, than is likely to arise

81

from the comparison of the different schools of expression. Interesting as are technical differences, they do not touch us so deeply as those subtle spiritual differences, those delicate sentiments and moral senses portrayed in fine works of art. In the same way any author hopes to gain more sympathy for the wisdom in his thought than praise for the style of his writing.

The harmony experienced when we find others thinking and feeling as we do, creates a deeper bond between us than any likeness of the flesh or fashion of behaviour. Ethical thought and feeling sincerely cultivated by each in his own sanctuary, must lead to closer union among men, and check the tendency to fight over modes, and the history and classification of modes, and the relative values of each, which lead to such endless and profitless preaching and pride.

Is not every lover charmed by the uniqueness of his maid ? There is no one ever like our best friend ; his individuality is the chain that binds our affections.

CHAPTER VI
THE TRANSIENT NATURE OF MODES

CHAPTER VI : The Transient Nature of Modes

I
t would seem hardly necessary to call attention to the transient nature of modes, seeing how new materials and methods of manufacture, new tools and fresh conditions are of almost daily occurrence : but for the fact that there yet remain certain elements that change not, like certain kinds of stone, which by their nature have dictated certain forms of architecture, as for instance stone found in large sizes lead to the lintel and column treatment, while smaller stones called for the arch. These are what we may term enduring qualities. Timber, like all natural substances, has its possibilities and its limitations, which endure from generation to generation, and a reverent nature will always respect, if not rejoice, in these limitations. Other materials there are the limitation of which we are only partially acquainted with. Possibly iron

is one of these. We do not know the length of life possible to iron with any certainty, under all conditions, therefore the modes of expression in that material are still developing. It is obviously unwise under these circumstances to tie the architect down to any style of the past. If the Tudor arch is still the most graceful and still the most frank avowal of practical needs, and best fitted to the material nearest at hand, and meets all requirements and conditions of modern life, why not adopt it and use it if need be in conjunction with the round arch or the lintel, if either of the latter can be justified on the same grounds. But the traditionalist is shocked by what he calls the mixture of styles. Fitness does not appeal to the mind already wedded to definite modes of expression. The fact that the two forms of arch were seldom, if ever, used together in ancient times, blinds his eyes to the fact that altered conditions of modern life, may demand the consideration of requirements non-existant in previous ages. The individualist is always ready to cast off the shackles

86

of a bygone time, and is willing to meet the needs of the present, while still holding fast to all enduring qualities.

The plea for harmony should not be used as a weapon to close the eyes to fitness, though it is an essential quality in all good modes, to be preserved by a loving sense of reverence for Nature's fundamental conditions. As when the builders added to Westminster Abbey each in the manner of his own time, and so greatly increased our interest to-day in the differences in style. The modes vary considerably, but the spiritual expression shows a loving reverence and devotion to truth, justice, honesty, candour, generosity, humility, order, loyalty and dignity. And in these qualities we have a sublime harmony. There are those that will fail to admit this, because their minds are dominated by the material qualities of the different styles of each period. The variety in the mode of expression takes precedence before the thoughts and feelings expressed. Their attention is so rivetted to forms and features peculiar to the

87

different periods that attention to non-material qualities does not occur to them. They are the disciples of formulæ. There are others similarly constituted who cannot materialize in their minds any combinations of requirements and conditions without primary reference to known examples. If it is a Town Hall they have to build or a public bath, they must refer back to some ancient temple, and impose modern conditions and requirements upon their design. The concrete form with them must precede the final conception, while others of the individual type will evolve the final concrete form, out of thoughts and feelings quite intangible—building, as it were, the material out of the spiritual, from within outwards, rather than from without inwards. This last type must, of course, be affected indirectly by memory of existing things. But there is a wide difference between the influence of memory not deliberately referred to, and the determined espousal of a pre-existing design.

What you can remember is your own, what you sketch you steal.

When Pugin designed the Houses of Parliament, to meet the conditions of plan dictated by Sir Charles Barry, he used his memory, which was well stored with the best examples of Tudor architecture. No living architect of his time could compare with him for intimate knowledge of that style. You may search the Houses of Parliament from top to bottom, and you will not find one superficial yard that is copied from any pre-existing building. He adopted the forms most suited to the materials and requirements, and was governed by no pre-existing examples, but faithfully met, to the best of his knowledge and ability, all those requirements and conditions which were presented to his mind, classifying them and anointing them with his devout spirit, allowing his moral sentiments to play like dancing light on every detail.

Augustus Welby Pugin was indeed a truly devout individualist—and none the less a Catholic, a fact which debarred him from entering into the competition for the Houses of Parliament, which the Government of that

89

day decided must be built in the Gothic manner. And so it was that Sir Charles Barry, knowing nothing about Gothic, and caring less, employed Pugin for the work. In this way the Government imposed the Gothic principle, but not any particular Gothic style.

We have travelled some way on the road of tolerance since those days, and have widened the possibilities of individual development ; but, in spite of all advance, are we not much more collectivist and tyrannical ? Much more materialistic than spiritual ?

This example we have cited would seem somewhat to refute our arguments against the imposition of any style. On examination, however, it will be seen that the mode adopted by Pugin was one born and bred in England alone, thoroughly germane to the climate, and national in character, and not so very far removed in time from Pugin's own period. Hence the conditions of material and labour fitted exactly the mode of his design. He cannot be said to have been dominated by the style he ultimately displayed, for it was a natural growth out of novel conditions. In contrast to this, we have only to look at St. Paul's Cathedral to see the effect of a foreign example dominating and violating all conditions of climate, national character and material, the form being so unsuited to the material that added strength had to be given to the stones by hidden ironwork.

Fitness being a law of nature, we must respect and be continually striving to attain it. The more we search into the operation of natural law the more fit it appears to us to be. The struggle for fitness leads us to respect the natural qualities of things, and helps us to check self - assertion and avoid wasteful elaboration.

The desire for fitness involves an appeal to individual character and a menace to collectivism. We may glorify matter by adding our own spirit to it, our noblest and best thoughts and feelings, but how can we ever hope to improve the exquisitely perfect fitness of Nature ? Human expression must grow in power and glory with the march of the ages, but the fitness of nature is the same yesterday, to-day, and for ever.

There would be little or no attempt to over polish or stain materials, and fictitious appearances would not attract us, if we felt more reverence for natural qualities. The material native to a country is always more harmonious with that country than any importation. Unpolished oak, stone, brick, or slate agree with our climate, light, and national character far more than polished wood, marble and mosaic, but nevertheless associations attaching to material qualities which awaken fond memories, are accounted of greater value than the attention to nature's ordinances which we advocate.

Modes would not suffer the vagaries of fashion, or be subjected to the ignorant criticism of cranks if based more on the qualities innate in things, and such fundamental emotions as awaken general interest and sympathy.

CHAPTER VII : A Revolution

The revolution we desire needs no banners, bands, or bloodshed. It is the gentlest and quietest imaginable. What men believe has the most far-reaching and permanent effect on their characters, individually and as a Nation. That is to say, the effect is accumulative. Herein we see the real benefit of the principle of collectivism when allowed to operate naturally. How powerful are the prevailing beliefs of a people ? Our experiences in India are alone enough to teach this truth. And so the revolution that we wish for must rise up in the mind of each of us, and must not be forced upon anyone from without.

We need only to search diligently for indications of moral sentiment in all material things ; in all familiar objects of daily life, in the home, in the street, in the work place, where we play and where we pray.

No material object exists that will not convey some spiritual meaning to our moral sense, or recall one or more of the inner springs of action, if we only look for such tokens. The habit of looking out for signs of reverence, love, truth, justice, mercy, honesty, candour, generosity, humility, order, loyalty, and dignity in our own work and the work of others has many advantages. By this habit we are kept in constant remembrance of the unseen, and higher qualities of life : we are lifted by it above the material, not to despise matter but to value and use it more justly. We are helped also to be constructive rather than destructive, in our criticism ; we are schooling our minds to pursue the good, the beautiful, and the true, and are not encouraging the spirit of denunciation and revolt.

The pursuit of these sentiments as expressed by men in material things is the surest way to cultivate a just judgment. It shuts out to a great extent any prejudice we may cling to in favour of particular modes. It enlarges our sympathy, it admits into our sanctuary all modes that possess the same sentiments, and it makes us more mindful of the unseen. We then find material things holding a subordinate position in our minds while yet they are elevated by being recognized as the vehicles of the spirit.

The very poker at your fireside becomes of interest to you the moment you recognize the sentiments of its maker. Maybe its maker's mind was absorbed by greed, and apish imitation for greed's sake ; then will you find no grace, no truth, no dignity in your poker. It will be an ill-bred poker, and you will feel no joy in it. But if it is full of grace, and fitted for its purpose, just and generous in its proportions, candid, orderly, and dignified, will you not then feel friendly towards it, and the mind that shaped it ? So, too, with all the objects of daily use ; if we train ourselves to look for signs of moral quality we shall do much to encourage true culture and bring spiritual joy out of material mire.

We must believe that the beauties of nature are sent for more reasons than to please the eyes of poor man.

97

No one can doubt the educative value of visible beauty; therefore it would revolutionize our lives, if in all we produced and made we recognized the necessity of conveying some common moral sentiments.

How quietly it can be done and how profound and indelible is the effect. Instead of straining every nerve to imitate a foreign expression we should fall in more naturally with the endeavour to express individual emotions, and be absolutely sincere. Thoughts and feelings that are common to all would more readily be conveyed than those feelings which are strange and foreign.

The interest we feel in the spiritual significance of things depends on our own degree of spiritual development, and must act as a powerful check to purely sensuous enjoyment. Sensuous experience can only quicken the faculties, they cannot refine the mind. But the search for evidence of emotion does exercise the moral sense and tend to elevate the mind, making us cry out for beauty and joy, and spiritual life in our homes and in the street.

98

We should be taken out of ourselves, and real healthy individuality would become the generally recognized condition of mind, instead of the exception. This method of regarding the material world as capable of administering as much to the spirit as to the flesh, if not more so, would be found fascinating to all degrees of intelligence, and would stimulate human sympathy and interest and make many dull industries break forth in fresh vigour and new songs of praise.

The very remembrance of our better nature at the moment of creative effort has a spiritual effect on our work, quite impossible to measure in its importance but none the less real.

Who in his travels has not come across some fragment of ancient art that has appealed to him with winning eloquence, and sent a thrill of warm sympathy through his veins. It is the thought of the man that made it that is so transmitted ; it is not any material quality in the object. It cannot be handled or conveyed to another. What is it in music that stirs our spirit ? Is it not something far more godly than

99

the vibrations of ether ? What is it in poetry that penetrates to the innermost sanctuary of our nature ? Not words alone. It is, and was, and ever will be the unseen that is the glory of the seen. Matter can have no purpose if it be not to manifest the spirit : to convey the thought and feeling, which we all prize, more than anything else. If this be a fact of our nature, it must follow, that matter in any way affected by man must partake of and reflect his spirit, his thoughts and feelings. We recognize this in the Cathedral— why, then, not in the lamp-post ? If we all sought for thoughts and feelings in the objects around us, it would spare a vast amount of heartache, which we now feel if we are ignorant of names and dates. Men often fear to express individual taste lest they should betray some lack of the knowledge of so-called styles. We often hear the remark, " Art is not in my line," or " I know nothing about art," as if art consisted in a settled mode, or order of mechanical actions, which had to be practised like the contortions of the acrobat. Collectivist notions

has led to this dividing up and parcel-
ling off of groups, and materialism
has set its hateful seal on each, so that
the modes espoused by each body of
men figure in the mind as if they had
no common qualities at all; we want
the different groups to feel their interdependence much more than their
independence. We want the business
man to feel that beauty is as needful
to *his* moral and spiritual well-being
as it is to any other kind of worker;
that *his* qualities are adequate for the
creation of beauty; and that no man
is born without adequate qualities for
the creation of beauty unless he be
born mad. Not that all have capacity
for technical skill, to paint or to carve
or to build; but all have the moral
sentiments and power to stimulate
and impart them, without which no
picture, no statue or building could
ever be produced. And there are,
after all, the most vital and the most.
precious qualities in all human production.

In our intimate study of technique
and materialistic examination of old
and venerated examples, we have come

to think of tangible qualities alone; and all the sentiment and glory of songs without words, and thoughts without matter, have ceased to charm us out of our smug, contented materialistic mood. The evidences of our worldly prosperity have grown so gigantic that it has blocked out the view of our horizon and hidden the rising sun of spiritual light.

Our plea for the intangible cannot form any excuse for careless or imperfect work. Technical excellence must still be regarded as necessary to truth, accuracy, and fitness. The desire for fitness is the parent of the practical mind, therefore the fitting of ideas to things and making matter demonstrate our thought and feeling is only making things more fit. The more closely we look into the question of ideas in things the more regard must we pay to individuality: for as we differ one from another in the degree of our sensibility to thoughts and feelings, we naturally seek those things which manifest the sentiments most dear to us. This diversity opens the door to the wide world. We rejoice to find men of all degrees of culture and sensibility, so that artists and creators of all sorts and degrees may find their sympathetic patrons. It fills the breast with hope and admiration. Dark and dreary are the clouds of fashion and formality, and the collective energy of conformity that threatens the sunshine of free thought. When modes are made to tyrannize over man's secret emotions, when collectivists drive us to smother our innermost feelings and concentrate attention on material qualities — then does individuality suffer, and the spirit dies of starvation. Sincerity, which is essential, becomes almost impossible.

Hold fast to moral sentiments, look for and read them wherever you go, and in the silence of your work let them be eloquent.

We need no street corner stump oratory, no ranting or raving, for the citadel we have to take is within our own breasts. Happily we need not fear wounding the susceptibilities of any one. It is a private affair.

The expression of moral sentiments

by individual effort is only to be observed by loving sympathy : it is not a force that offends, but the music of the gods, heard only by the godly.

CHAPTER VIII
ON THE PRACTICAL APPLICA-
TION OF ETHICAL IDEAS

CHAPTER VIII : On the Practical Application of Ethical Ideas

In all creative work of a material nature a regard for truth may be manifested by a frank admission of our requirements and conditions; this candour will save us from waste of energy and useless elaboration of innumerable details. A home suited to limited means need not assume the airs and graces of the more wealthy, but should court simplicity, which always commands respect when coupled with thoroughness and candour. For the poor man, one living room may be far more homely and attractive than many apartments, provided the fear of confessing poverty does not prompt him to use all manner of subterfuges. Fear is a very hard taskmaster, and answerable for many a lie. If only we could love truth more we should fear less.

If we could set our hearts on proclaiming nothing but the truth about ourselves, the fear of public opinion would vanish, standards of fashion would cease to exist, and our homes would then be furnished only with what we needed for daily use : and each object would have to be as beautiful as we could make it or procure it, in order to harmonize with our feeling, rather than with an assumed convention.

Love of truth would lead us to a more candid avowal of practical construction and check us from disguising it, or the materials of which it is made. Sham arches and columns that carry nothing but disgrace would be drummed out of existence. Stone shells would no longer hide the iron embryo of architecture. Broken pediments and symmetrical facades would cease to satisfy us. Architecture learnt on the drawing board and measured off by the yard would be delegated to the world of Academys and collectivism. We should grow to love the natural qualities of materials. Oak, because it is a native tree, would be used in its natural colour ; no attempt would be made to make it appear old or like other woods. Wall papers and floor-cloth would not be made to imitate tiles or marble. Nothing fashioned to look better than it is, would be tolerated. Hidden parts of houses would not be made shabby in order to lavish more on the exposed places. The pursuit of truth will drive us to preserve our credit and not have one quality for the back and another for the front, as it was once expressed, " Queen Anne in front and Mary Anne behind."

There are semi-detached houses where the front doors are so placed that one owner appears to own both houses, the whole front flanking his door on either side, while the other tenant has his door carefully hidden round the corner ; in this way it is hoped to trade on the lie that one tenant is affluent enough to inhabit twice as much as he really possesses. To a mind bent on truth, such a scheme would be impossible.

As the fireplace is the eye of a room to which you look and gravitate as to the embrace of a friend, so it should be clear, open, frank and large, deep set if you will, but simple and true, not clogged with innumerable surfaces and textures, not low down and blinking up at you as the glance from a snake. No slit surrounded by surfaces at all angles, glittering glazes and gaudy metals, but all as broad and simple as the human eye setting, which carries the mind to the centre and rivets the attention on the iris as the window of the heart within ; so should the fireplace of a room carry your eye quietly to the flaming embers.

The doors, too, may partake of the qualities of a good host, hospitable and free in their ample width, yet invested with vertical lines to suggest dignity and grace. An entrance hall cut up with many materials and varied surfaces will not suggest breadth, repose, or order. Confusion and restlessness and fatigue are the inevitable result of walking over polished marble wood, and wool alternately. The sense of order conveyed by breadth of surfaces and reposeful arrangement do suggest qualities akin to faithfulness, frankness, simplicity, and self-control.

When the sun sets horizontalism prevails, when we are weary we recline, and the darkness covers up the differences and hides all detail under one harmonious veil, while we, too, close our eyes for rest. What, then, is obviously necessary for the effect of repose in our houses, if not to avoid angularity and complexity in colour, form or texture, and make our dominating lines horizontal rather than vertical. A well-balanced mind is reposeful, so a well-designed house must be reposeful too. We may cut up our homes as we cut up our thought, with multifarious mixtures of mental pictures and emotions hurriedly forced through our consciousness, so quickly that no lasting impression is made and no joyous feeling is aroused. The mind is so satiated instead of fed.

Confusion and elaboration are often used to hide inferior material and workmanship, and create a fictitious effect of value and richness. Greed and untruthfulness make this manner of work, and these dominating forces swamp all higher feelings. No art that is mainly inspired by the desire to make money can benefit our better nature ; it can only minister to our bodily needs. Only a love of beauty and the expression of moral sentiments, can impart to things, that quality which will make them minister to our spirits. And there is nothing material, that is needful for the flesh, that cannot be made an instrument of spiritual culture at the same time to some degree.

The habit of mind which leads to the classification of our faculties in water-tight compartments is very ancient. The church has encouraged us to separate our religion from our life, and bind it in creeds and dogmas and illustrate it in material, which we designate as ecclesiastical, and any attempt to introduce features familiar in the church into our family apart-ments is now resented by most people. The spirit is regarded as an intruder if caught affecting the business affairs of everyday life. Commercial depart-ments are carefully guarded against spiritual influences. The artist who tries to inspire a little love of beauty is smiled at as a faddist or fanatic, dangerous to the working of the mill.

The separation of the instinct of self-preservation, from the creative spirit, that is to say, generally speaking, the desire to get and the desire to give, are both forces only perfect in effect when properly balancing one another. Both are needful to the development of character, and therefore must be cultivated by the individual. It is wrong that any one of us should assume that either field of activity is more his sphere than the other. It is the combination of the two forces of spirit and matter, commerce and art, science and religion that go to build up character and strengthen individuality. This happy blending of our nature is to be encouraged in a million ways; most important is it then that we should break down all barriers that stand in the way, and convince each living soul that he has been invested with faculties for his full development : that no moral sentiments are bestowed on one and wanting in another.

The village mason performed his ritual when he carved the demon on the doorway of the church, quite as truly as the priest at his prayers inside. In those days Gothic tracery adorned our houses ; now the water-tight compartment principle has ruled such features out of touch with our lives, except on Sunday. To get back to a more spiritual activity, it is suggested that the ideas of the unseen should permeate the seen, and while we are striving to create beauty we shall be stimulating the appetite for it in ourselves and in each other. And all those who are not directly engaged in creative art are equally helpful if they too truly desire and seek the same.

We do not naturally value simplicity in ourselves. To have travelled and seen much, to be versatile and cosmopolitan in our tastes and complex in our behaviour is, to most people, more attractive than simplicity of character and conduct which, to acquire in these days, needs strong will and independent thought ; in fact, all the self-reliance that we can muster. To strive to cultivate simplicity has a very powerful effect on character, and is quite comparable with sympathetic regard for modern conditions.

We need not live in mud huts and dress in woad to be simple, nor need we live on nuts. The instinct of sincerity will regulate the impulse to be simple, and few qualities can we find that are more far-reaching in effect on mind and matter than this one dictate " be simple." Anyone setting this law before himself will at once feel the necessity for humility ; he cannot indulge in a flourish of trumpets and a dazzling display of rich detail. He will find that the fewer the elements of his work the more carefully they have to be proportioned, and the more pure and perfect each has to be. Like any simple melody, its parts must perfectly support the whole. So in architecture or pattern design, each item must lend lustre to the rest and flow harmoniously throughout.

This process of building up with desire to be simple, makes a very strong call on individual feeling. The sense of proportion. being one of temperament far more than learning and education, one of feeling far more than thought, will, if sincerely exercised, stamp any work of art with that character that is the unique possession of its author. It should be a spontaneous expression, and never deliberately formularised. When a designer consciously fixes a scale of proportion for his own use it becomes a mannerism and eccentricity, appearing like self-advertisement, when all the while it should be as unnoticed in its birth as our own voices are to ourselves. Or when proportions are borrowed, all personal quality is hidden, and the work strikes us as commonplace, and without life, interest or distinction. The mathematician's maxims of Greek proportion leave us starved and cold, as if in the presence of death.

In music we find the law of simplicity frequently broken as it is in architecture, and human vanity delights to have it so. To understand the complexities that few can grasp, and admire the incomprehensible seems to lend lustre to our apparent intelligence. There is a kind of glutton's delight in dwelling in rooms with examples of every nation's feeling and every people's thought. The in-

116

ebriation that kills dull care has its
attractions. Let the debauched artistic
appetite live in a museum if it will.
But when we are considering the
formation of character and the encouragement of individuality, we must
search out the true principles that
make for improvement. It is not our
business to discover means of delight.
All forms of happiness must be regarded as consequences, not as ends
in themselves, and if this be accepted
as a true fundamental principle, it
will go far to simplify our lives and
strengthen personal character.

Look up at our great public buildings and ask yourself how much you
could spare of their details without
suffering any loss. And it will be found
that the myriad of dust catching
details, are not the parts that convey
any feeling of any value whatever
but are like notes thrown in to add
complexity and muddle the brain, so
that the relation of parts so ill-con-
sidered may not be observed. In like
manner elaboration is useful to hide
defects. Rich looking wallpapers hide
poor-looking pictures.

Reverence is shown by our treatment of the natural qualities of materials, as well as by pointed arches and vaulted isles, and may be expressed by our frank admission of conditions and requirements. Reverence might almost be described as the mother of dignity, for the dignified have all first learned to respect something higher than themselves before they have been respected. And dignity is surely the state of mind desiring to be worthy of respect—something we can look up to, hence it is associated in the mind with height and verticality. This we can impart only when we sincerely feel it. But height as such will not carry us far, otherwise some American architecture would be the finest examples of dignity. It must make a vast difference to the effect we receive from any building, whether it has been raised to minister to man, body and soul, or whether it has been piled up to fill his pocket.

Love, justice, mercy, and generosity are qualities that must be felt by those who would seek them in the works of man—each and all may chant songs

118

of praise in stone as much as in story. Our buildings, our books, and our furniture cry out at us for shame! When greed has ground down every worker and drowned justice and mercy beneath its arrogant elaboration.

The sacrifice of enrichment and display, or even accommodation in order to gain greater perfection in secret places, and care for servants instead of costly carvings, are the directions in which much can be done to establish the character of generosity.

Concentrated ornament will help us towards making that ornament finer and more effective, as well as assisting towards the improvement in the quality generally. The building covered with indifferent decoration invariably exhibits a sacrifice of general quality. Structural parts are cheapened to pay for gaudy display. A sense of order which precedes and follows from punctuality and precision, and inspires faith, can be conveyed even in the arrangement of a tradesman's notice. One simple type instead of many will show a steadiness that reminds us of a reliable man, it is orderly and controlled, simple and frank, not decked out with flourishes and formed with varigated proportions. Why, if we have any information to convey, should we seek to dazzle the eye and satiate the brain? Like the modern shopkeeper, who thinks he can charm the buyer by exposing all his wares at once.

Material matters have developed at such a pace it is hard to avoid being swept along with the tide. To be mindful of more than the needs of the flesh when shopping, is most difficult to the average mortal; so much is studiously prepared to intoxicate and bewilder the higher instincts. The sense of beauty which is common to all is carefully poisoned at the fountain head by our early training in modes. Our knapsack of knowledge has one small compartment into which certain examples of the beautiful are placed, and these we take out on our travels and compare with what we meet in order to formulate our judgment. The process is like the mechanical stone crusher, it destroys the heart in everything that falls beneath its weight.

We have thus grown to rely on museums as essential for the poor who cannot travel.

With what result. Is the peasant work of to-day to be compared for spiritual beauty with the work of the thirteenth and fourteenth centuries ? It is not the experience of travel that quickens the spirit, but experience of thought and feeling. We have relied too much and too long on material things. Museums full of unused articles divorced from the purpose of their being, are like the mausoleums of matter. Oh ! departed voices, still audible to the sympathetic spirit, what intense joy might we not feel, if we could but thrill with the sentiments that gave you birth, and drink deeply beneath the substance of your being until we, too, are intoxicated with the same emotions.

We must be generously disposed before we can impart to matter that quality which will keep it alive in our affections. The beam must look strong enough for its task as well as be so. The thin, skinney mullions with cotton like lead glazing suggest only meanness.

Generosity can only show in our work when we are forgetful of our own gain, and bursting to bestow the best that is in us, and glory in straining every nerve towards perfect feeling and fitting expression. The generous love of beauty will prompt attention to the meanest detail. To the generous mind no detail is too small, or too insignificant to be worthy of our efforts to make it beautiful. The bestowal of grace is a devotion as much when manifested in the kitchen as in the cathedral.

It is only a desire for gain or praise that makes us classify our works and regard some as big and others as little, and important and unimportant with the various intermediate degrees, and gild the parts that show and leave the others shabby. Whereas the old monks carved to the glory of God in hidden places, content to have given their energy in generous devotion. The longing to bestow may be encouraged until we forget to think whether our offering is deserved or not, and surely this is a blessed state of mind to be in ? When we cease to sit in judgment on

men and things, and absorb all our
energies in adding something of
worth wherever we go. The little
dash of overweight the grocer will
throw in to your pound of sugar is
sweeter to him and to you than ten
times the cost of it. We can all add
our dash of sweetness where we will ;
that drop of spiritual tonic which is
never paid for in any material, is just
the essence of eternal hope that keeps
us striving for a better state. It is the
love in man that preserves his identity,
while stretching out to help his fellows,
and this same love is the fundamental
principle of man's nature, abstraction
as it seems to be ; every breathing
animal knows what it means. We
cannot think of a creator without this
same quality to give the personal
element to our conception. We may
talk of the " absolute," but we cannot
worship the " absolute " unless we
invest our idea of it with that personal
affection. However much we think that
we are the product of our ancestors
and the result of external forces, we
cannot get away from the consciousness of the ego which is manifested

by our affections, and we feel the impulse to love to be the divine gift of a power antecedent and ever constantly working within us. But never does this feeling for one moment destroy our conviction, that our own affections are peculiarly our own. And this consciousness makes us feel the value of individuality. Personality is the one quality we never desire to part with, and would never agree to change. We may covet a man's conditions, and even his mind. Both his thought and feeling we would sometimes exchange for our own, but we hold fast to our identity. That little something, however small it may be, we may call the soul. It establishes the idea of individuality and identity, it is the one grain of real distinction that we cannot do without. And for the glory and preservation of this ego we are bound to be very introspective: very careful not to be sucked into the vortex of collectivism, or stained by the corrosive canker of materialism.

CHAPTER IX

DISTINCTION, NOTORIETY AND POPULARITY IN THEIR RELATION TO INDIVIDUALITY

CHAPTER IX : Distinction, Notoriety and Popularity in their Relation
to Individuality

We are all more or less the
product of our time, and it is
impossible to measure the
extent of our own freedom, either of
mind or body. Each man's conscience
will tell him the actions he is respon-
sible for, and establish without doubt
our modicum of independence in certain specific cases. But we, nevertheless, recognize the difference between
distinction, notoriety, and popularity,
and that each depends upon a different
kind of personality. The notorious
man may never be popular and the
distinguished man may never be
notorious. The murderer is sometimes
notorious, but seldom distinguished
or popular. The great soldier is often
distinguished and popular, but not
so often notorious. It would seem that
we reserve the term " noted " for those
persons who have performed one or

more " noteworthy " actions. They may be good or bad, the extent of the notoriety may depend on circumstances quite beyond the control of the noted. The act may be one appealing to the sentiments prevailing at the time, or a person may become notorious quite against his will, by force of circumstances often accidental. It may or may not be quite independent of personality, as, for instance, if anyone fell from a Royal train in rapid motion without being hurt he would, doubtless, be notorious for a while. And so we find popularity depends much more on personality than notoriety ever can do. To be popular we must synchronize with our times, we must sympathize with the thoughts and feelings of the multitude, we must catch the temper of the moment and harmonize with popular sentiment. In a materialistic age we have to make matter our first concern. Good business habits and good bargaining will count for more than ethical qualities. The successful architect to-day is not the spiritual leader and raiser of popular taste, but he who can minister most smoothly to the thirst for ease and comfort, and teach men how to multiply material gain. Making things look better than they are is sure to be amply rewarded by a people grown indifferent to truth and shy of sincerity.

It is obviously desirable that in this world we should have both classes of mind, the man whose mission it is to harmonize with his time—the mind alert to seize the dominating sentiment and minister to it with all his might. We could not get on at all but for this amiable, obliging and most useful class. But let us not regard such qualities as all-sufficing, or forget the quality that gives distinction. To act according to popular sentiment, and in accordance with generally accepted principles, as a collectivist and orderly conformist, is a common attitude quite distinct from the individual, who sets up in his own mind certain fundamental principles and guides for conduct, accordingly. He may be quite mistaken in his ideas of what are fundamental true principles, but he deserves respect for sincerity,

129

as long as he remains true to whatever his principles may be. Most fanatics are worthy of respect on this account, but opposition to the aims of the fanatic will often outweigh and obscure any lingering respect for his sincerity.

The truly distinguished are always those who act from an inner conviction of fundamental principles, and they must always be sincere individualists. They are acting from within outwards, more than from without inwards, and it is the amount of reality in their conduct that gives them distinction. This is beyond the reach, and quite outside the pale, of collectivism. No collective forces can possibly produce what we rightly understand by distinction. Collectivism may furnish opportunity for the display of such qualities, but in no sense can it produce them. Sincerity is the quality most conspicuous in the distinguished, and, as we have already proved, the least encouraged by collectivism. It is the one instinct of all others that checks the collectivist, and makes it possible for him to act sometimes for good.

Distinction is a term too often lightly used, as when we speak of a woman distinguished for beauty, or a man distinguished by his size, any difference, in fact, from the general, is in some degree distinction, but it is easy to detect that we are speaking on a material plane exclusively when we use the term in these connections. When we speak of Wellington as a distinguished soldier, we are not thinking of his figure or his nose, but of his personal character, his sincerity to fundamentals, and loyalty to the verities of life and death.

It would create a pleasing change in popular sentiment if we could encourage distinction more than popularity, and tempt our Chancellors of the Exchequer to cease thirsting for the latter. Popular applause is such an alluring poison that we have ever been guilty of—the insane adage " Vox populi, vox Dei." Many a poor character has been led into the valley of unfaithfulness by the fascinating cry of public opinion. To please a crowd is a temptation that few can resist when it comes. Only the strictest vigilance of individual character will enable us to keep our hands and hearts clean, and only through faithfulness to ourselves can we be really useful to others. It is a fatal mistake to set out to please a multitude. The good comedian does not so proceed, nor the bishop, nor the King, or general. One and all act on principle, which they regard as of fundamental importance, and all alike feel the importance of sincerity to those principles. Lesser minds will scorn the idea of being guided by any principle, feeling that custom, ancient history, dogma, and authorised rules of behaviour are much safer guides to conduct. The collective opinion of the multitude is more reliable, and so they become controlled from without rather than from within. Both class of minds may be equally sincere, and equally honest. But the effects on character produced by these two distinct methods are of the utmost importance. And hence it is we seek to show that by encouraging the individual to look for the signs of ethical ideas in material things, he will thereby attain spiritual culture and true distinction, and the joys of life will become more rich and fruitful. Life will be more beautiful, and our influence more acceptable.

CHAPTER X

INDIVIDUALITY AND THE
PRESENT WAR

CHAPTER X : Individuality and the Present War

To denounce the present war as wicked and deplorable is to be like children in their nursery crying out against the punishments inflicted by their parents. Is it not more manly to deplore the wrong thinking that has made necessary the chastisement of war? We cannot attribute this war to the wilful wickedness of any one man. It must be the evolution of many causes and effects, and the operation of many just laws. The cause of our trouble is not the war. War is the *effect* of wickedness.

Our trust in the faithful fulfilment of natural law strengthens our position as men. We feel our personal share in life more clearly defined the more distinctly we recognize fundamental laws. Our individual sense and responsibility is not weakened, but strengthened, by the recognition of the mighty forces of nature, and we grow to recognize the consistency in the two beliefs, in predestination and free-will, both hand in hand and mutually helpful.

We know for a certainty that every wrong thought has got to be corrected, and that countless ills ensue until it is cast out. It is a necessary part of our freedom that we must suffer for our mistakes. By thinking wrongly we establish a false philosophy, and gradually accumulate forces in a wrong direction, until now we see whole nations, or many nations, fast falling into trouble by the materialism grown out of wrong thinking.

The sanctity given to dogma by the claim of Divine authority, has had the effect of drawing some thoughtful and sincere people out of the field of religion altogether. One detected error in our idol is enough to turn the heart to stone, and the mind is quickly directed from the spiritual to the material. Untruth is always working mischief, and in the spiritual sphere more than in any other. The heart in search of truth and in love with it, cannot harbour a lie in the name of

138

religion. Absolute sincerity is essential to the individualist; he will not deliberately deceive himself even if he could. And hence in their perplexity many have turned their attention to the things of the flesh, and worldly prosperity and material progress has been the result. But there comes a time sooner or later when the conviction grows, that in this life matter and spirit are essential to each other.

Each individual soul has to learn that he must do his own thinking for himself, he must balance the spiritual and material forces in his own nature. If he relaxes his efforts, he will find himself sucked into the stream of conventional opinion, and swamped in the whirlpool of superficial thought; where collectivism is ready, like the reeds and the rushes to entangle his feet, and drag him under. Every system of philosophy must be brought before the bar of each man's reason, conscience, and love. It is a personal matter that each individual is bound to look after for himself—no collective organization can do it for him. We can help and encourage each other to

Lightning Source UK Ltd.
Milton Keynes UK
UKHW022252011021
391519UK00005B/1102